WHO NAMED THE PLANETS?

Discovering and Naming Planets

Astronomy Beginners' Guide Grade 4 |
Children's Astronomy & Space Books

BABY PROFESSOR
EDUCATION KIDS

First Edition, 2020

Published in the United States by Speedy Publishing LLC, 40 E Main Street, Newark, Delaware 19711 USA.

© 2020 Baby Professor Books, an imprint of Speedy Publishing LLC

Baby Professor Books are available at special discounts when purchased in bulk for industrial and sales-promotional use. For details contact our Special Sales Team at Speedy Publishing LLC, 40 E Main Street, Newark, Delaware 19711 USA. Telephone (888) 248-4521 Fax: (210) 519-4043.

10 9 8 7 6 * 5 4 3 2 1

Print Edition: 9781541959545
Digital Edition: 9781541962545
Hardcover Edition: 9781541979536

See the world in pictures. Build your knowledge in style.
www.speedypublishing.com

TABLE OF CONTENTS

When a baby is born, one of the first things to be done is to give the baby a name. There are many reasons why people choose to give a baby a certain name. Sometimes, a baby is called after a relative or another person as a form of honor. Perhaps the name is chosen because it sounds nice or the person giving the name, usually the parent or parents, simply liked the name!

Choosing a name for a baby boy.

It is not only people who are given names, planets and other celestial objects are too.

It is not only people who are given names, planets and other celestial objects are too. This book will discuss how the planets received their names. Then, the book will provide interesting facts about each planet to see whether it 'lives up" to its name.

CHAPTER ONE:
WHO GETS TO CHOOSE A NAME?

People have been looking up at the heavens and naming stars, planets, and constellations for millennia. (Millennia is the plural form of millennium, which means one thousand years.) People from all over the world, from different cultures, and with different languages all have their own history with the night sky.

Ancient astronomers stargazing.

Before widespread higher education, name of stars were simply carried on by word of mouth.

Before the ability to read and write was common, before widespread higher education, these names were simply carried on by word of mouth, or oral tradition. However, as technology improved and cultures started interacting and more people became literate, there were some problems. People would have many ways of spelling the same star name.

Sometimes people would get confused because there were several different names for the same star, or there would be the same name for different stars! As a result, to avoid confusion and to encourage astronomers from all countries to work together, the International Astronomical Union (IAU) was formed!

A group of people watching the stars at night.

IAU General Assembly in Prague, Czech Republic, in 2006.

The International Astronomical Union

The IAU was founded in 1919. It came together so that discoveries about celestial objects could be made aware to scientists all over the world. Today, thousands of professional astronomers are a part of the organization.

Logo of the International Astronomical Union

The IAU has many purposes. It is a part of the International Science Council and it tries to promote international cooperation with Astronomy research. It also helps to promote education about Astronomy. It is probably most famous for having two groups called the Working Group for Planetary System Nomenclature (WGPSN) and the Working Group on Star Names (WGSN). It is these groups that decide the internationally recognized names, and spellings, of stars and planets.

Logo of the International Science Council

The IAU tries to promote international cooperation with Astronomy research.

The star at the end of the tail of the Ursa Major constellation has been known by two popular names, Alkaid and Benetnasch, but the IAU WGSN has chosen the more common alternative of Alkaid as its official name.

Naming Planets

The IAU takes naming celestial objects very seriously. The process is not simple. The organization must make sure that the names are respectable, non-offensive and that no object has two names. Also, the names of celestial objects should not be business names or names for pets. The names cannot be too long, sound too much like another name, or be unpronounceable.

When naming newly discovered planets, the IAU will first give the planets a number which is called its designation. In addition to taking the time to ensure that the planet has not been previously discovered, the IAU makes certain that enough is known about the planet to find its location again. When all of this is done, the IAU will work to decide a name.

LYNX

2

15

21

10

ALSCIAUKAT (31)

MACULATA (38)

ALVASHAK (α)

Lynx constellation with the names of basic stars

The discoverer is given the honor of proposing a name and explaining why it has been chosen.

The process can take years, with many names being taken into consideration. In addition, the discoverer is given the honor of proposing a name and explaining why it has been chosen. Names from history and mythology are popular. However, no event that happened in the last century should be referenced. In the last few years, the IAU has even allowed the public to vote on names for new planets.

There are some other traditions as well. Satellites, objects that orbit other objects, like moons, are often given a name that relates to the name of the object which they orbit. For instance, the moon, Triton, which revolves around Neptune, is so named because in myth, Triton is Neptune's son. New planets sometimes are given a name based on the Sun around which they revolve. There are many minor planets and, as a result, there are expected limits on how many can be named at a time.

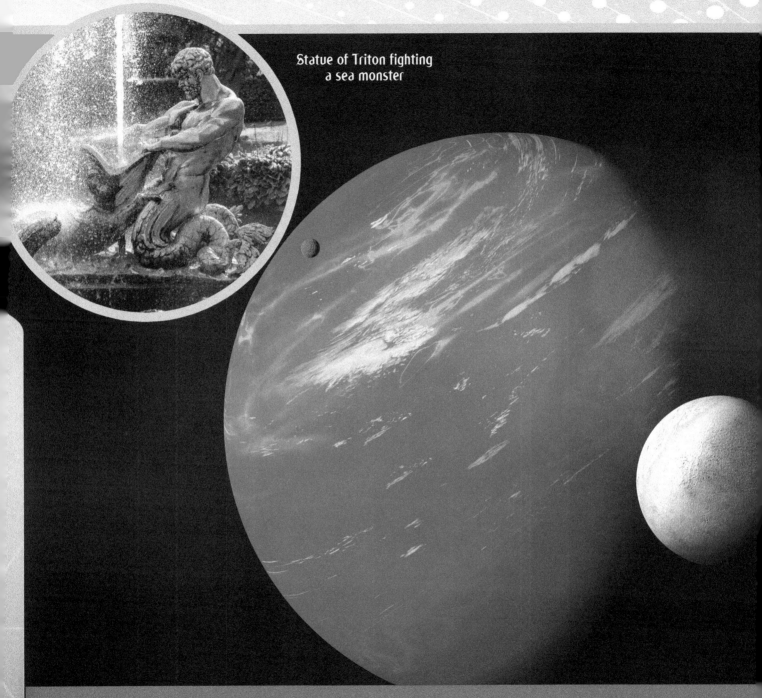

Statue of Triton fighting
a sea monster

Planet Neptune with its moon Triton

Ancient Greek astronomer studying the stars at the observatory of Alexandria.

Naming Stars

Naming stars is, perhaps, even more difficult than naming the planets. Stars are much more numerous and much easier to see in the night sky. Many cultures have had many traditions regarding stars and constellations, (patterns and collections of stars.) In addition to that, many historical astronomers have named the same stars different names.

The problems that can be caused were observed even before the founding of the IAU. Different astronomers tried to come up with different systems that would work universally. Johann Bayer in the 17th century tried to organize stars by order of brightness in a constellation. This had some problems as sometimes it was hard to tell which star was brightest. Also, he would run out of Greek letters to use to label them. Still, his method remained popular for about two hundred years.

The constellation Orion, illustration from an edition of Johann Bayer's Uranometria.

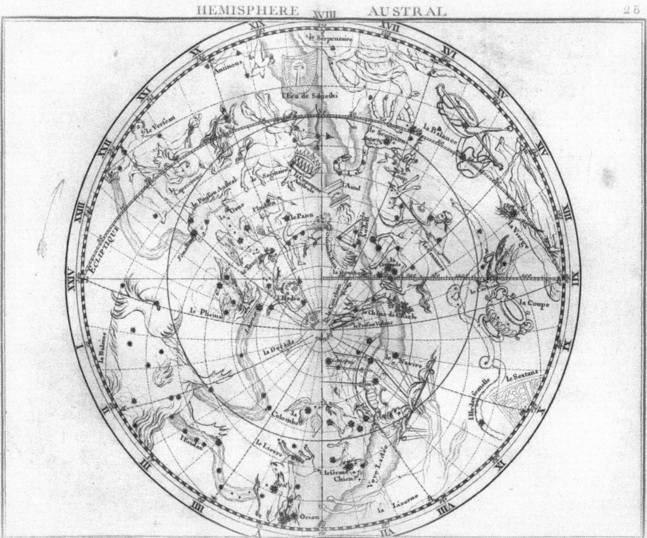

The Celestial Atlas of Flamsteed (1795)

Other schemes were introduced afterwards. The most well-known were by Flamsteed and Lalande who numbered stars by right ascension in a constellation.

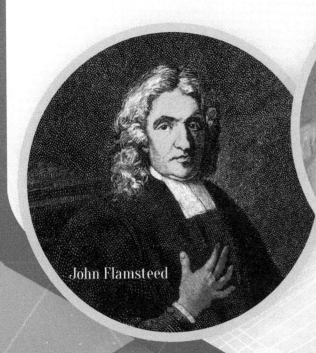

John Flamsteed

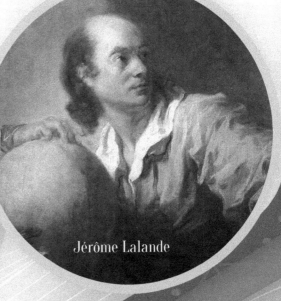

Jérôme Lalande

Finally, Benjamin Gould would try to improve this method. Few people use this method today, however. The issue is not entirely resolved. Additions have been made to these methods and stars are labelled by order of discovery as well. As of 2016, the IAU has been working internationally to properly catalog these star names. Until very recently, even famous stars had no consistent spelling or formal names.

Benjamin Gould

Some companies have offered to allow you to buy the right to name your own star.

While some companies have offered to allow you to buy the right to name your own star, the catalogs they keep are not internationally recognized. Another reason for the new push to name stars is that as technology improves, space exploration is more viable. Names capture the imagination. The stars can be seen by all people, and the IAU helps to make them tangible. There is also an effort to make sure that star names from all the star-gazing cultures around the world are recognized.

CHAPTER TWO:
THE NAMING OF THE PLANETS

While the IAU has officially named many planets, it did not name the planets that are in our solar system. The IAU formally recognized the Latin names that had been used in the Roman empire for millennia. These names were taken from Roman Mythology, which had its roots in Greek Mythology. Even the name planet, meaning "wanderers," has its root in the Greek language. These names are steeped in ancient history.

Planets of the Solar System

MERCURY

Mercury

Mercury is the Roman god of messengers, travelers, and thieves. He was said to have winged feet and a winged helmet. He could move very quickly. Since Mercury is the closest planet to the Sun, it can orbit the Sun faster than any other planet. It is believed to be for this reason that Mercury got its name.

Statue of Mercury, the Roman god of messengers, travelers, and thieves

Venus

Venus is the brightest planet we can see in the sky. Venus was the Roman goddess of love and beauty. It is suspected that the planet was named for her because it was the brightest planet known at the time. Venus has sometimes been called the morning or evening star since you can see the planet at sunrise and sunset.

Statue of Venus, the Roman goddess of love and beauty

VENUS

EARTH

Earth

Earth is unique in being the only planet not named for mythology. It gets its name from the German or English words meaning ground or dirt. Likely we named the planet Earth because it is the ground on which we stand. Ironically, Earth is 70% water.

Our moon is simply called the Moon, because for a very long time people simply did not know that other moons existed.

Earth's moon is simply called the Moon.

Mars

Mars is a bloodred planet and this is most likely why it was named after the Roman god of war, Mars. The moons of mars were named for the children of Mars' Greek form, Ares. Phobos and Deimos were the Greek gods of fear, panic, and dread.

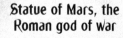

Statue of Mars, the Roman god of war

MARS

JUPITER

Jupiter

Jupiter is the largest planet in our solar system so it should come as no surprise that it was named after the king of the gods. Also, as the first of the gas giants, and a notoriously stormy and windy planet, it is no small irony that Jupiter was the god of the air, sky, and lightning.

Jupiter had many affairs and many children. Many of his moons are named after these characters from the myths.

Statue of Jupiter, the god of air, sky, and lightning

Saturn

Saturn is the furthest planet that we can see without a telescope. Saturn was the Roman god of agriculture. This works nicely as Saturn is the color of ripe grain.

Saturn was the father of Jupiter. It is also possible that Saturn was so named because he was found behind Jupiter, his son. Saturn was known to be a cruel father who ate his children until he was taken down by Jupiter. Hence, Jupiter is the king and at the front.

Statue of Saturn, the Roman god of agriculture

SATURN

Surface landscape of Saturn's largest moon called Titan

Saturn has many moons, but the largest is called Titan. Titan means big, which is appropriate as Titan is larger than Mercury. Titan can also mean great achievement. With a dense atmosphere and vast amounts of surface liquid, it is highly unique. Titan refers to the fact that Saturn and his siblings, as the predecessors of gods, were called Titans. Another moon was named for Saturn's wife, Rhea.

Uranus

Perhaps to continue the tradition of placing displaced fathers behind the sons who fought them, Uranus was the father of Saturn. He was the Roman god of the heavens which, once more, suits the color scheme, as Uranus is a light blue-green color. Uranus was also guilty of eating his offspring and Saturn overthrew him.

Statue of Uranus, the Roman god of the heavens

URANUS

Miranda   Ariel   Umbriel   Titania   Oberon

Uranus has 27 known moons

Cordelia	Cupid	Titania	Prospero
Ophelia	Belinda	Oberon	Setebos
Bianca	Perdita	Francisco	Ferdinand
Cressida	Puck	Caliban	
Desdemona	Mab	Stephano	
Juliet	Miranda	Trinculo	
Portia	Ariel	Sycorax	
Rosalind	Umbriel	Margaret	

Uranus has five major moons:
Miranda, Ariel, Umbriel, Titania, and Oberon

The names of Uranus' moons

Uranus' moons are unique in that they are not named for mythological people or creatures. Instead, they are named after characters from the writings of William Shakespeare and Alexander Pope.

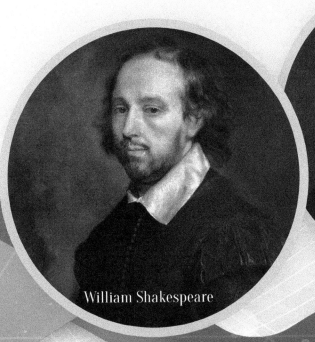

William Shakespeare

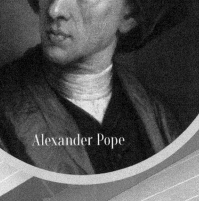

Alexander Pope

Neptune

Neptune was the Roman god of the sea. It is quite likely that Neptune was named because of its blue color. Neptune was also one of the most powerful gods of Ancient Rome. The moons of Neptune were named after other people and creatures from the ocean in Roman myths.

Statue of Neptune, the Roman god of the sea

NEPTUNE

PLUTO

Pluto,
The Dwarf Planet

The naming of Pluto is quite interesting. Pluto was named by an eleven-year old girl. She suggested the name to her grandfather who passed it on to the appropriate people. Pluto was felt to be suitable as Pluto was the god of the underworld. Being the farthest planet away from the Sun, the name seemed appropriate. It also fits because Jupiter had two brothers, some of the most powerful gods, Neptune, and Pluto.

Statue of Pluto, the god of the underworld

Ironically, astronomers would later come to realize that Pluto was not a proper planet. Its gravity was not powerful enough to be the dominant force in the area, which was necessary for a planet. In the old myths, Pluto was forced to go down to the underworld and was generally barred from gathering formally with the other gods. How very appropriate, then, that Pluto would prove to be a dwarf planet.

Pluto with Proserpine and Orpheus in the underworld.

Charon is the largest of the five known moons of the dwarf planet Pluto.

Pluto's largest moon is named Charon after the minor god that ferried the souls of the dead to the underworld. It was also an indirect reference to the name of the discoverer, James Christy's, wife, Sharon.

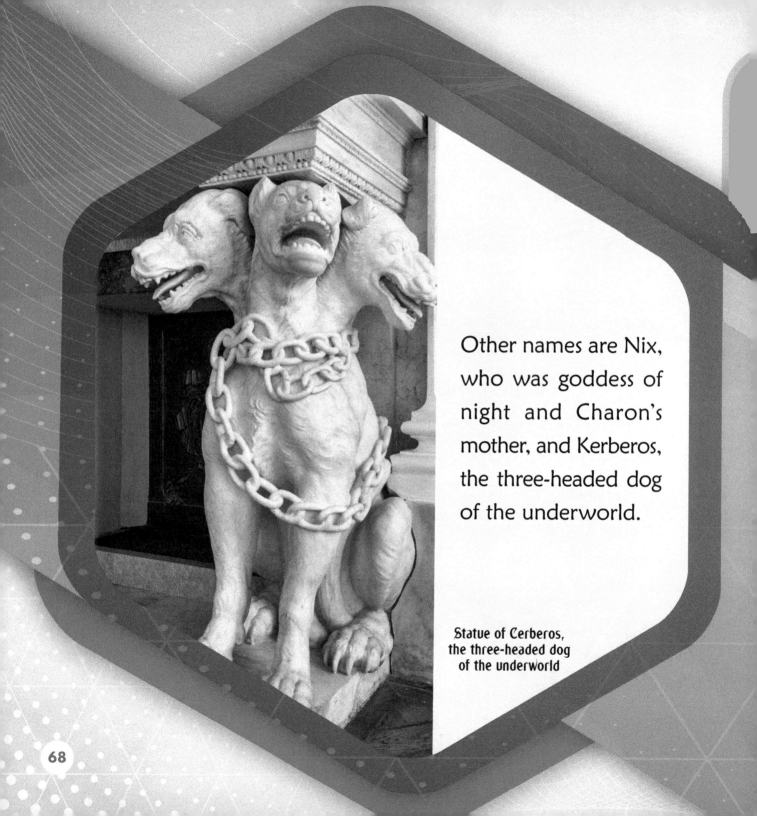

Other names are Nix, who was goddess of night and Charon's mother, and Kerberos, the three-headed dog of the underworld.

Statue of Cerberos, the three-headed dog of the underworld

Asteroid Nix, satellite of Pluto

The Universe is a vast place and there are billions of stars. Humans have been fascinated by the stars and planets for millennia. Now, as international cooperation grows, it has become increasingly important that there be a common way of labeling and naming these celestial objects. This is handled by the IAU which decides on the formal names, makes sure that there is consistent spelling, and that there are no duplicate or inappropriate names. To learn more about Astronomy, Cosmology, and much more, look for more Baby Professor books!

Lightning Source UK Ltd.
Milton Keynes UK
UKHW050643270722
406443UK00002B/40